THE AFRICAN COMPANY PRESENTS RICHARD III

BY CARLYLE BROWN

★

★

DRAMATISTS
PLAY SERVICE
INC.

NOTE ON BILLING

Anyone receiving permission to produce THE AFRICAN COMPANY PRESENTS RICHARD III is required to give credit to the Author as sole and exclusive Author of the Play on the title page of all programs distributed in connection with performances of the Play and in all instances in which the title of the Play appears, including printed or digital materials for advertising, publicizing or otherwise exploiting the Play and/or a production thereof. The name of the Author must appear on a separate line, in which no other name appears, immediately beneath the title and in size and prominence of type equal to 50% of the size of the largest, most prominent letter used for the title of the Play. No person, firm or entity may receive credit larger or more prominent than that accorded the Author. The following acknowledgments must appear on the title page of all programs distributed in connection with performances of the Play:

Originally produced in 1987 by Penumbra Theatre Company
Lou Bellamy, Artistic Director.

Produced by Arena Stage, 1992,
Douglas C. Wager, Artistic Director;
Tazewell Thompson, Director.

SPECIAL NOTE ON SONGS/RECORDINGS

Dramatists Play Service neither holds the rights to nor grants permission to use any songs or recordings mentioned in the Play. Permission for performances of copyrighted songs, arrangements or recordings mentioned in this Play is not included in our license agreement. The permission of the copyright owner(s) must be obtained for any such use. For any songs and/or recordings mentioned in the Play, other songs, arrangements, or recordings may be substituted provided permission from the copyright owner(s) of such songs, arrangements or recordings is obtained; or songs, arrangements or recordings in the public domain may be substituted.

2

THE AFRICAN COMPANY PRESENTS RICHARD III was originally developed and produced by Penumbra Theatre Company, "Minnesota's Only Black Professional Theatre Company" (Lou Bellamy, Artistic Director), in St. Paul, Minnesota, in February, 1988. It was directed by Lou Bellamy; the set and lighting designs were by Ken Evans; the costume design was by Deidrea Whitlock and the sound design was by Ben James. The cast was as follows:

STEPHEN PRICE..James Harris
HANNAH PRICE .... Bernadette Suyllivan
SARAH ....Rebecca Rice
ANN JOHNSON ....Faye M. Price
JAMES HEWLETT .... Terry Bellamy
PAPA SHAKESPEARE ....Marion McClinton
WILLIAM HENRY BROWN ....James A. Williams
THE CONSTABLE-MAN..................................... Mike McQuiston

THE AFRICAN COMPANY PRESENTS RICHARD III was produced by Arena Stage (Douglas C. Wager, Artistic Director; Stephen Richard, Executive Director), in Washington, D.C., on December 9, 1992. It was directed by Tazewell Thompson; the set design was by Douglas Stein; the costume design was by Paul Tazewell; the lighting design was by Allen Lee Hughes; the sound design was by Susan R. White; the production manager was Dennis A. Blackledge and the stage manager was Wendy Streeter. The cast was as follows:

STEPHEN PRICE...Jed Diamond
SARAH ....LaDonna Mabry
ANN JOHNSON ....Gail Grate
JAMES HEWLETT ....Leon Addison Brown
PAPA SHAKESPEARE .... Wendell Wright
WILLIAM HENRY BROWN ....Jonathan Earl Peck
THE CONSTABLE-MAN... David Marks
MEMBERS OF THE CONSTABULARY .... Ed Eaton,
                                                                        Paul Niebanck

THE AFRICAN COMPANY PRESENTS RICHARD III was produced by The Acting Company (Zelda Fichandler, Artistic Director; Margo Harley, Executive Director), at the Bardavon 1869 Opera House in Poughkeepsie, New York, on January 15, 1994. It was directed by Clinton Turner Davis; the set design was by Douglas Stein; the costume design was by Paul Tazewell; the lighting design was by Dennis Parichy; the sound design was by Fran Sutherland; the dialect consultant was Ralph Zito; the production manager was Daniel L. Bello and the stage manager was Chris De Camillis. The cast was as follows:

STEPHEN PRICE .... Matt Bradford Sullivan
SARAH .... Shona Tucker
ANN JOHNSON .... Kelly Taffe
JAMES HEWLETT .... Allen Gilmore
PAPA SHAKESPEARE .... Chuck Patterson
WILLIAM HENRY BROWN .... Cedric Harris
THE CONSTABLE-MAN .... Richard Topol

PAUL LAURENCE DUNBAR (1872-1906)

WE WEAR THE MASK

We wear the mask that grins and lies,
It hides our cheeks and shades our eyes —
This debt we pay to human guile'
With torn and bleeding hearts we smile
And mouth with myriad subtleties.

Why should the world be over-wise,
In counting all our tears and sighs?
Nay, let them only see us, while
    We wear the mask.

We smile, but oh great Christ, our cries
To thee from tortured souls arise.
We sing, but oh the clay is vile
Beneath our feet, and long the mile;
But let the world dream otherwise,
    We wear the mask!

                (1895)

CHARACTERS
(In Order of Appearance)

STEPHEN PRICE
SARAH
ANN JOHNSON
JAMES HEWLETT
PAPA SHAKESPEARE
WILLIAM HENRY BROWN
THE CONSTABLE-MAN

SETTING

New York City, circa 1821

THE AFRICAN COMPANY
PRESENTS RICHARD III

ACT ONE

Scene 1

THE PARK THEATER

STEPHEN PRICE. Ladies and gentlemen! Ladies and gentlemen, please! Please ladies and gentlemen, may I have your attention, please.... Ladies and Gentleman for those of you who don't know me, my name is Stephen Price. I am the manager of the Park Theatre. I have been so since 1809 and now, tonight, it is my burden to tell you on behalf of the proprietors, John's Astor and Beekman, how deeply we regret this unfortunate delay in tonight's performance. I am here to assure you that, that disturbance outside is fully under control. The constable has informed me that the culprits who caused this riot, are locked inside the Eldridge Street Jail House and will not be released, until they swear, in blank verse, never to play Shakespeare again. Perhaps some of you think these deliberations harsh. But the performance of this "Black" Richard, right next door in the City Hotel was meant to be a direct affront and challenge to the Park Theatre. The African Company thought it was throwing down the gauntlet. Slapping the Theatre in the face, reproducing this great play we present for you tonight, as a cheap spectacle and a tasteless novelty. Ladies and gentlemen, understand me, we live in a country that is young and wild and doesn't even know its own thoughts. But in here ... in here the lights through which you see me are the brand new patent oil lamps, hung in three chandeliers with fifteen lights in every one. There are twenty-six hundred seats in here and the gallery is as big as a barn. In here. In the Park Theatre the show starts on time. We bring before you some of the greatest actors of our age. The stars and darlings of the English stage. George Cooke, Henry Wallack, Edmund Kean, Tom Cooper. And tonight, for the first time in America, this curtain will rise on The Tragedy of King Richard the Third with Junius Brutus Booth. Not ungreat achievements for a theatre in a country not yet fifty years of age. There are those of you up there in the third tier. Prostitutes soliciting customers. Fingersmiths, picking through people's pockets. You people from the country with your apple cores and your pippin and cabbages in your trousers, just ready to discharge on the heads of the poor people down here in the pit. I want you to look under this arch and through these portals down on these boards and see for yourselves that anything is possible here. That success can be yours. That the future is only a footfall away. And you Negroes up there in the gallery, free men and women in an America full of slaves and slavery. Even you must see that something splendid is happening here. These imitative performances of the African Company were an ungrateful arrogance. But I assure you ladies and gentlemen, it will never happen again. And now, ladies and gentlemen, for your pleasure, The Park Theatre presents, The Tragedy of King Richard the Third.

Scene 2

SARAH.   One and two-three. One and two-three, one and two-three. One and two-three. No, no, no. One and "then" two-three. Here, try it like this. One, two, three. One, two, three. One, two, three. One, two, three. One, two, three.... There, that's better.
ANN.   Why we got to be countin' all the time?
SARAH.   'Cause the countin' takes the place of the music.

ANN. The countin' takes the place of the music? How can countin' take the place of music? Well, I tell ya Sarah, by the way you countin', that's some mighty funny music. Where you learn this dance at? What you call this again, Sarah?

SARAH. Waltz. It's a waltz honey. Mrs. Van Dam teach it to me today. That's what I was doin' at work today. I was waltzin'.

ANN. And what was you waltzin' with Sarah? A mop and a broom?

SARAH. No, I was waltzin' with Mrs. Van Dam. Lord, child, that old woman is crazy. She like to drive me out a my natural mind. She got nothin' to do all day, but follow me 'round the house. She call herself helpin' me. "Let us cook dinner, Sarah," she says. "Do you think we should wash the windows?" "Why don't we dust the sitting room." And then she just sits there watchin' me work. Talkin' and talkin' and talkin' herself blue in the face. Poor thing is so lonely. Today she tells me how she and Mr. Van Dam went to this great big ball and oh how they waltzed. I said, "What's a wall-zza?" She said, "No Sarah dear, waltz." So I asked her how do it go. And before you know it honey, there I was dancin' in the sittin' room with Mrs. Van Dam.

ANN. Speakin' a dancin'. You wasn't out in the African Grove after the play last night, was you?

SARAH. No. How, what happened?

ANN. Folks was out strollin' as usual. Walkin' all saditty like. Sashayin' up and down the African Grove, like them Negroes thought they was kings and queens, dukes and duchesses or somethin'. But Shakespeare come and make 'em step out them Sunday attitudes. Poundin' that drum a his. Slappin' on that thing like there was no tomorrow.

SARAH. Shakespeare? That old fool. He was drunk, wasn't he?

ANN. No he wasn't drunk. But he was a reelin' honey. Had his neck down and his head cocked to the side with his shoulders rolled up like so. Ba-ba-boom-de-doom, ba-ba-boom-de-doom, ba-ba-boom-de-doom, ba-ba-doom. Eye-whites was red as cow peas. Eyeballs rolled back up into his head and he was

9

a swayin'. A-ba-boom, a-ba-boom, a-ba-boom. Sarah, it was like he had just stepped right out a life itself and was looking around at it, like it was a dream he was dreamin'. Them Negroes who before was prancin' up and down the African Grove like a flock a peacocks, start to trip and stumble. And it seem like the only thing that kept 'em all from fallin' down was the sound a Shakespeare's drum. Ka-boom, ka-boom, ka-boom. And just like that folks start to dancin'. Dancin' like they was runnin' from death. Dancin' all wild like.

SARAH.   That old Shakespeare is a fool, I tell you. Throwin' them bones and rattlin' 'round talkin' crazy. Talkin' that talk, what he call African talk. People be 'fraid a that old man, you know. With his garlic bulbs and black cat bone, scare people to death. Lot a them people is just ignorant. Some of 'em just come up from slavery. Some of 'em ain't nothin' but Africans just off the boat from out the jungle. People like that. That crazy old man gets them people all excited.

ANN.   Still, it ain't no reason for the Constable-man to come and try and take up Shakespeare's drum. Come talkin' 'bout, "Cut out all that noise or I'll lock you all up! Stop that darn music!" Shakespeare didn't even hear that man. He just keep on playin', and them people they just keep on dancin'. And when he raise up his club to hit on Papa Shakespeare's drum, Billy Brown jump up and grab hold of 'em.

SARAH.   Grab hold a who?

ANN.   The Constable-man. He grab hold a the Constable-man.

SARAH.   No, he ain't lay his hands on no Constable.

ANN.   Looked him in his eye, like I'm lookin' at you. Told him, say, "Don't you break that drum. That drum is all he has. He's gonna stop playin' it, just don't you hit that drum." Well it got so quiet out there, you could hear a mosquito's wings flappin'. And then all of a sudden it was like Billy Brown had become invisible to that man. He just walked away from Billy like somebody had put a spell on him. Started shoutin' and wavin' his club in the air. Nobody payin' him no never mind. Folks just started creepin' off down the streets like ghosts feedin' the shadows. And Papa Shakespeare, he still there with his eyes rolled up back in his head, pounding on that drum a his.

SARAH. They wild Annie, they wild. Billy Brown and that Shakespeare is wild. And Shakespeare, he don't have but one lick a sense. Babblin' like a nigger with all a his "dis and dat and dey and where ya gwine and how come ya for ta come na so." I believe he think he be sayin' somethin' with all that mumblin' and carryin' on. They suppose to lock ya up for drumin'. Drumin' against the law.

ANN. What you suppose to do is help ya friends when trouble come. That's what ya suppose to do. Jimmy ain't lift a finger.

SARAH. Jimmy?

ANN. Me and Jimmy was sittin' underneath that big 'ole poplar tree, dangling our feet along, watchin' the whole thing. And he ain't move yet.

SARAH. Oh, so it's danglin' along with Jimmy now, is it?

ANN. Oh Sarah, I like Jimmy you know. I really do. But he can act so dog gone highfalutin'. Talkin' his high flown, fancy English. "I will not be a part in that nonsense. Nonsense. Silly nigger nonsense." But that was nonsense with names. Names like Billy Brown and Shakespeare.

SARAH. Jimmy was just actin' sensible, what it sound like. And if ya want to listen to me, you better off dangling with Jimmy Hewlett than with the wild likes a Billy Brown.

HEWLETT. *(Off-stage.)* Hello!

SARAH. That's him there now, ain't it? *(Enter Hewlett and Papa Shakespeare.)* Hello Jimmy.

HEWLETT. Hello Sarah. Hello Annie.

ANN. Hello Papa Shakespeare.

PAPA SHAKESPEARE. Hello Annie. Hello Sarah.

SARAH. Hello Shakespeare. How are you?

PAPA SHAKESPEARE. Oh, the body I well. And you Sarah, how the body?

SARAH. My body is my business Shakespeare. Well, Jimmy Hewlett, you sho' did yourself some play-actin' last night. Didn't he Annie?

ANN. He was all right.

11

HEWLETT.   All right?

SARAH.   And didn't he look good. Them girls was up in there just a clappin' and shakin' they handkerchiefs at him before he even said anything. I like the way you be breathin' heavy. Liftin' up ya chest like it's about to bust. Then you sing it out just a fillin' the room. And them girls don't care what he sayin', long as he just keep on talkin'. Ain't that right Annie?

HEWLETT.   Now Sarah, you don't stop that you gonna make blackness blush.

PAPA SHAKESPEARE.   And Jimmy know he doin' it too. He havin' a good time. He step over here and then he look, so. Then he walk over here and he look again. Then he talk some with the audience and he parade back, like so. He walkin' like a hunch back, but he paradin' so, "A horse!" he say, "a horse! Me whole world for dis horse!"

SARAH.   Listen who's rememberin' lines.

PAPA SHAKESPEARE.   How, you say me don't know me lines?

SARAH.   You may know 'em, but can't nobody hardly understand that man Catesby in this play by the way you say 'em.

PAPA SHAKESPEARE.   It don't matter how I talk. It's what I say, what you want to be listenin' for. I can recite them lines from Shakespeare so they make you weep.

SARAH.   Make who weep? Make me weep? What you gonna make me weep over? Make me weep recitin'? No, you ain't gonna make me weep. Not by recitin' you ain't. Why you can't hardly even read.

ANN.   Sarah.

SARAH.   Well, it's true. He don't understand what he sayin'. He can't read.

PAPA SHAKESPEARE.   Billy Brown read 'em to me. Read 'em sailin' board them packet boat. Black Ball and the London Liner. We did it all the time. How you think Billy get money to hire this whole house to be a theatre? We got great big pockets in our coats. Oh yes, Blackman carry cargo too, ya know. Billy carry dis book a Shakespeare's stories. And Billy read 'em to me and he doin' all a the parts. The kings and the queens and the little fairies and the Moors. Like that Moor, Aaron what got the white woman. And the Prince from Morocco what tryin' to get the white woman. And Othello what lossin' the white woman ... I say Jimmy, why my brother William always puttin' the black man with the white woman. We better not do them stories in here.

SARAH.   Well, if you know 'em so good, how come you don't do Catesby that way. Go on, let us hear you say some recitin'.

PAPA SHAKESPEARE.   I can recite many things my brother William say. And can say 'em so sweet, they be like dem same sounds he was listenin' for, when he wrote 'em down. But ya just want to laugh to hear the way I say 'em. So no, I don't want to talk.

ANN.   Sarah, you hurtin' Shakespeare's feelings. Not that Jimmy Hewlett would have anything to say in his behalf.

HEWLETT.   Annie, did I do something to upset you?

ANN.   Not at all. I hadn't given you a thought until now.

HEWLETT.   Annie, you're acting very peculiar.

ANN.   I'm not acting. You the one who is the actor.

HEWLETT.   And what's wrong with acting? Colored folk act all the time. You and Sarah pretend you're maids. You even play the mothers to some other people's children. We all charade the great role of the happy, obedient Negros advancin'. What is that, if it ain't acting?

PAPA SHAKESPEARE.   And de whole world is de stage.

HEWLETT.   The whole time I was working as George Cooke's man-servant and his dresser, he could never tell if I was playing a part or not. 'Cause as great an actor as he was, he performed from night to night, while we perform all the time. I remember one night the old fool was playing King Lear. He didn't like Lear. Could play him a villain, but it shook him in his bones to put on Lear's robe. We were standing in the wings, waiting on his cue, and he turns to me and he says, "Hewlett, you're a Negro. What's it like for you to suffer?" Quick in my mind come what I really want to tell him. But instead I told him, I said, "Well sir, we feel like we been doin' so much with so little for so long, we feel we can

13

do anything with nothin'." And he looked at me and he thought about it for a while, and he laughed and he said, "Hewlett, it's a damn shame they won't allow you to go out on that stage with me. You could be Lear's fool. You'd be perfect for the part." And I knew, and I knew he knew, that, that was me out there underneath Lear's robe, while he bowed to applause for a Lear that he could never again be. A Lear that tore the whole house down. (*Enter Billy Brown applauding.*)

BROWN.   Bravo, Jimmy, bravo! It be just like the paper say.

SARAH.   The paper?

BROWN.   Yes girl, we in the paper.

ANN.   We in the paper?

BROWN.   Ain't I say so?

HEWLETT.   Well read it. Read it to us, man.

BROWN.   "Hung Be The Heavens With Black Shakespeare." ... "In the upper apartments of a hired house on Mercer Street some colored citizens of this city are demonstrating their native genius and the vigorousness of their imaginations with nightly presentations of William Shakespeare's *Richard the Third.*"

SARAH.   Wait 'til Mrs. Van Dam hear this.

BROWN.   "Mr. William Henry Brown, the proprietor mise en scene, has spared neither time nor expense in rendering these entertainments agreeable to ladies and gentlemen of color. How delighted would the Bard of Avon have been to see his Royal Plantagenet performed by a fellow as black as the ace of spades. A dapper, woolly-headed waiter, who serves supper at the City Hotel. The audience was of a riotous character, that amused themselves with throwing crackers and gingercakes on the stage. Lady Ann was played by a lady named Ann. A lovely looking Negress, who played the part with the royal rage it required. The person of Richard, performed with more than a plausible imitation, was on the whole, histrionically correct. Several fashionable songs were sung in most excellent taste and style and except for the arrest of Catesby, who was taken up by the watch, the affair was lawful and orderly. Moreover, this sable group which calls itself the African Company, have graciously cordoned off a partition in the back of their house for the accommodation of whites."

SARAH. Ooo, that's the part I wanna hear 'bout.

BROWN. "This vexatious gallery, has of late been filled to overflowing by whites who come to criticize and ridicule, but remain to admire and cheer these ebony interpretations of the Bard."

ANN. Billy Brown, you sure got you a lot a nerve ...

HEWLETT. Let me see that paper.

SARAH. ... and Jimmy, you sure was right when you said, colored folks would pack up in here to see a Black king. In a king's robe and crown. Sword hanging off his hip, velvet gloves on his hand and the spurs on his boots ringin' and echoin' in the hall. "A horse! A horse! My kingdom for a horse!"

HEWLETT. "... was on the whole histrionically correct." "A plausible imitation."

ANN. Don't pay that any mind, Jimmy. That man don't know what he's talkin' 'bout. Sound to me like he just like the sounds a the words he's writin'.

HEWLETT. Some fat, powder-face Englishman can be an African Moor, but let the Royal Plantagenet be "as black as the ace a spades" and it's "a plausible imitation."

BROWN. Well, listen to you. Seems to me that just the other day you was just a little woolly-headed waiter in here. You ain't the same Jimmy Hewlett I seen here, come sneekin' into America.

HEWLETT. Sneekin' into America?

BROWN. Yeah, it was you. It was the first play-actin' I ever seen Jimmy do. He disguisin' heself as a sailor, sneekin' off that boat to keep from goin' back to that sugar plantation. He say, no more sugar island for Jimmy Hewlett, no sir. He practice long time to get them white folk to think he was no run-away. But when I first seen him, disguise or not, he didn't look no more like a sailor than a jay bird look like a duck.

HEWLETT. I couldn't walk.

BROWN.   You couldn't walk. I was lookin' right at him. I said to myself, now there's a Negro tryin' to escape.

HEWLETT.   I guess you could see me comin' with your eyes shut.

BROWN.   Had to teach him how to walk. Walk like a sailor. With big beamy strides and short, sturdy steps like the ground might swell up underneath ya like a giant rollin' sea and knock ya down. Walk like you was free. Straight up and tall and not lookin' 'round for nothin'. And then, I seen Jimmy become kind of a playwrighter. A playwrighter creatin' the character of James Hewlett. Free Negro, born in Rockaway Island, New York City. Singer, Shakespearean imitator, disguised as a man-servant and a waiter. Jimmy is tricky. You tricky Jimmy, you tricky. He got the people thinkin' he's a man-servant and a waiter.

HEWLETT.   The critic in this paper, eats his supper in the same hotel where this little wholly-headed waiter works. The next time he wants his mutton peppered, I'll pepper it for him. And I'll pepper it good and hot. And for Saturday night's performance, we go show him how 'e go so. Now, I thought this was suppose to be a rehearsal. Billy, you got the prompt book.

BROWN.   Yes sir, Mr. Hewlett.

HEWLETT.   Give it to Sarah, please. I want you and Shakespeare to carry the coffin. Annie.

ANN.   Yes Jimmy.

HEWLETT.   Act one, scene two. All right? You're walking across this way. From up here down. Now you don't have to say "obsequiously lament" Say, "While I awhile away lament."

ANN.   "While I awhile away lament"

HEWLETT.   Right. And don't say ... "untimely fall of virtuous Lancaster," make it, "The untimely fall of this sweet man."

ANN.   "The untimely fall of this sweet man."

HEWLETT.   Good. Now, remember he's your father who you loved more than life, more than slaves love freedom. Murdered. Butchered for a whim. You're walking behind his hearse. Slowly. Quivering with grief so heavy you can barely

stand-up beneath it. You stop. Now, tell the bearers to set him
down.

ANN. "Set down, set down your honourable load,
If honour may be shrouded in a hearse,
While I awhile away lament
The untimely fall of this sweet man ..."

Scene 3

THE STAGE OF THE PARK THEATRE

THE CONSTABLE. "To be or not to be. That is what we
must ask. Perhaps it is nobler in the heart.... No, no. in the
mind? In the mind to seek riches and fortunes. And by ...
and by ..."

PRICE. Good evening Constable.

THE CONSTABLE. Good evening?... Oh, good evening Mr.
Price. I didn't see you there. Have you been standing there
very long.

PRICE. Long enough. Are you looking for a new profession,
Constable?

THE CONSTABLE. Oh no sir. Not me. I could never be an
actor. I'd rather knock heads with the gangs in the Five
Points district, than be on stage. Why, I'd be frightened to
death, standing up here with all those people looking at me.

PRICE. Still, you seem to fancy the theatre. Are you sure?

THE CONSTABLE. Yes sir. Quite sure, sir. Although I love
your plays. I really do.

PRICE. You do? Well, thank-you Constable, but they're not
my plays. I simply put them on.

THE CONSTABLE. Just the same sir, I do. And this play
you're putting on Saturday night. *Richard the Third* with that
Brutus gentleman. I wouldn't miss it for the world. I'm going
to see it for free, you know. The Park Theatre is going to be
my beat that night, sir.

PRICE. Oh, you know the play?

THE CONSTABLE. Oh, yes sir. I saw it right here, on three

different occasions. Once with Mr. Cooper. Another time with Mr. George Cooke playing the part. Oh, he was great. And again with Mr. Kean. It was in the old theatre, before the fire. That was my beat up there in the gallery. Buzzard's Roost, the coloreds call it. From down here it certainly looks a long way away.

PRICE.   That must be rather a rough job up there, Constable.

THE CONSTABLE.   They're a rough and noisy lot, all right. But I manage to keep 'em in line. The gallery isn't bad. What's bad is after I leave the theatre, I've got the African Grove beat, 'til midnight.

PRICE.   Just the same, I think you'll have your work cut out for you. We've sold every seat in the house. And the gallery and the third tier pay at the door. They'll be a mob up there.

THE CONSTABLE.   Oh, I think you'll have a quiet gallery that night, sir. They've got their own "Black Richard" noising up Mercer Street. The African Company they call it. All the coloreds'll be there, I suspect. I hear that the other night, there were so many whites in there, that they had to put up a partition in the back. Can you imagine that sir? Making a partition for whites in the back of a Negro theatre.

PRICE.   Yes, I read the reviews. I don't understand why you boys down at the station don't seem to want to nip that in the bud. This African Company strikes me as a situation that's prime for trouble.

THE CONSTABLE.   You think so sir?

PRICE.   I think so, Constable. I think so. I really do. Don't you? Events like this always seem to come with a certain amount of hysteria. People are excited. Tickets are dear, the lines are long. Rumors and gossip abound. There's suspense on the streets. Anything can happen. Anything. The Park Theatre and the African Company, doing *Richard the Third* on the same night. People are bound to associate the two, and that can lead to trouble.

THE CONSTABLE.   That's what the watch is here for, sir. We'll see to it that it's a quiet, pleasant evening. The African

18

Company could never compete with the Park Theatre.

PRICE.   I don't care about the competition, Constable. Nor do I care about some poor imitative inmates of the kitchens and pantries, who are simply trying to entertain themselves. It's the peace that concerns me. A deeper, broader peace.... That spot where you're standing ...

THE CONSTABLE.   Here sir?

PRICE.   In the old Park Theatre, Constantine Leesugg stood right about where you're standing now, as Rosina in the world premiere of the English version of Rossini's *Barber of Seville.* Not the British or the American premiere, mind you, but the world. She was such a sweet singer and it was such a sweet song. It was a moment where everyone from down in the pit, high up to the gallery, had a taste in their mouths of what greatness was. That's what a backwards country like ours needs to come into the world. Not spectacles. Not disorder. Not riots. I only wish the members of the African Company under-stood. I wish there was some way to impress upon them the importance of what we're doing here on Saturday night. If only they weren't so enthusiastic. I bet those poor fellows haven't even read their fire code and keep that place over-crowded or without enough exits. Or worse. It could be a hazard. Anything can happen. Anything.

THE CONSTABLE.   I think I understand your meaning, sir. Maybe me and the fellows ought to take a look into it. Per-haps you're right, Mr. Price.

PRICE.   I am right, Constable. I know it.

Scene 4

PAPA SHAKESPEARE.   Last night at Billy Brown's African Theatre, in the play King Richard Three, I pretend to play a white man, name a William Catesby. And you know what happen? The Constable-man he come and take me away. They no say what I do. Maybe they arrest me for bad actin'. They lock me up in a cell in the Eldrldge Street Jail House. Put me in 'dere with a blackbirdin' slave ship captain. Didn't give me no bread nor water. And all that for Catesby. Tiresome little man, that they send 'round on errands everywhere for this man Gloucester, the King Richard Three. He's a strange man, this man, King Three. He always standin' there talkin', talkin', talkin' to hisself ... I mean, if we was back in de islands and you see a man there, standin' there, talkin' and talkin' to hisself. "Now is de winter of our discontentment, made glorious summer by dis sun a York" ... I mean, you would say this man is crazy, standin' over there talkin' to hisself. "And all de clouds that lowered over de house, in de deep bosom of de ocean buried." You would say, what is the matter with this man. He's sneekin about and rollin' his eyes, lookin' 'round; and ain't nobody 'dere. This the kind a thing for be madness. In the Jail House, I had me a dream. And in my dream, I was dreaming. When all of a sudden a great big ladder spring up from nowhere, set right down in the middle a the room. It's standin' up, straight up, stickin' up through the roof, way up in the sky, right on up, up through the clouds. Now, I don't know where that ladder leadin', so I wake me up. I don't want to be in dis dream. I got hard enough time being me, but I catch the devil being Catesby.

Scene 5

ANN.   Oh no. No. I don't see it, I don't. I don't see it a-tall. How, this man kills my husband and my father, and now I'm suppose to love him and turn around and marry him over a lot a sweet talk. Oh no, that don't make no sense. Then he goes and kills the woman afterwards. What I oughta do is take a stick to 'em. That's the story that should be in there. I don't mind that part where I call him a foul lump of deformity. When I cuss him down. That's when that story gets it right.

HEWLETT.   Good, Annie. Good. You suppose to be that mad.

ANN.   That's 'cause I am mad. I don't want people seein' me, goin' 'round thinkin' I'm the kinda person that would go for such a thing.

HEWLETT.   Is that what you're worried about? About people thinkin' you the same person as a part you're actin' in a play? Annie that's ridiculous. Nobody knows ya is gonna believe you gonna stand for that kind a foolishness.

ANN.   I can't do what you askin' me to do, Jimmy. I cannot be such a slack woman as this Lady Ann.

HEWLETT.   What's come over you Annie? What is the matter, all of a sudden? You were Lady Ann last night and the night before and the night before that.

ANN.   And it makes me mad every one a them nights, I'm actin' out such a huck 'em so woman as she is. Look what he says about her after she gone. "Was ever woman in this humour woo'd?/ Was ever woman in this humour won?/ I'll have her; but I will not keep her long." Now, what kind a mess is that? I have to look out after myself. Nobody takes care of me. I can't have people thinkin' they can woo me and humour me and take advantage of me like that.

HEWLETT.   Well, try not to think about what you're saying, just try thinking of the words.

ANN.   What else would I be thinkin' of? It's the words what make me mad. It's what they're about.

HEWLETT.   No, not the words and what they mean, but the sounds. The sounds they make in your ear. Like the huckster songs on the street. The woman selling hot soup on the corner. "Peppery pot, all hot, all hot!/ Makee back strong, makee live long/ buy my peppery pot." Or the crab man how he's shoutin', "Crabs, fresh crabs/ fresh Baltimore crabs/ put 'em in the pot/ with the lid on top/ here buy my Baltimore crabs." Good singin' crab man'll sell more crabs than one singin' bad. It's just like singing a song, all rhythms and rhymes. Ta-ta, ta-ta, ta-ta, ta-ta, ta-ta. Come on Annie. Please. Speak it with me. "Fairer than tongue can name thee, let me have some patient leisure to excuse myself."

ANN.   "Fouler than heart can think thee, thou canst make/ No excuse current but to hang thyself."

HEWLETT.   "By such despair I should accuse myself."

ANN.   "And by despairing shalt thou stand excus'd./ For do-

21

ing worthy vengeance on thyself./ That didst unworthy slaughter upon others."

HEWLETT. "Say that I slew them not?"

ANN. "Then say they were not slain./ But dead they are, and devilish slave by thee."

HEWLETT. "I did not kill your husband."

ANN. "Why, then he is alive."

HEWLETT. "Nay, he is dead; and slain by Edward's hands."

ANN. "In thy foul throat thou liest! Queen Margaret saw/ Thy murderous falchion smoking in his blood;"

HEWLETT. "I was provoked by her sland'rous tongue."

ANN. "Thou was provoked by thy bloody mind./ Didst thou not kill this king?"

HEWLETT. "I grant ye."

ANN. "Dost grant me, hedgehog? Then God grant me too/ Thou mayst be damned for that wicked deed!/ 0, he was gentle, mild, and virtuous."

HEWLETT. "The better for the King of heaven, that hath him."

ANN. "He is in heaven, where thou shalt never come."

HEWLETT. "Let him thank me, that help to send him thither;/ For he was fitter for that place than earth."

ANN. "And thou unfit for any place but hell."

HEWLETT. "Yes, one place else, if you will hear me name it."

ANN. "Some dungeon."

HEWLETT. "Your bed chamber."

ANN. You see. There you go again. This is the part that steams me. Any self respectin' woman would pull his eyes out. Kick him where he couldn't be knockin' on nobody's bedchamber no more.

HEWLETT. Annie, why did you stop? You're doin' it all right. You're supposed to be in a rage. That's what they said in the paper, remember. "Lady Ann, played by a lady named Ann, with the royal rage it required."

ANN. You right about that. That's what it calls for all right. A regular, royal rage.

HEWLETT. Yes, and while you played with the rage it

required, I was only "histrionically correct ... a plausible imitation." I don't see what you got to complain about.

ANN.   Jimmy, it's hard for me. It just is. It isn't easy for me, gettin' out them people's house every night. I got to work extra and make up for the time. And I can't tell them people where I'm goin'. They wouldn't let me out. I got to make up somethin' every time. Somebody's always sick or dyin'. It's a cousin' here or an uncle there. How much longer can I keep up that kinda lyin'?

HEWLETT.   Annie, if those people was to turn you out you can always get yourself another job. Nobody's gonna hire them Irishmen and Germans who come floodin' into New York every day to be no domestic. To be fashionably rich, the help has got to be black. In the last couple a nights Billy Brown has paid you more money than those folks you work for pay you all week. You can always be a chambermaid or somebody's nanny. Where are you ever gonna be a queen and not some servant, but right here, in this play with the African Company?

ANN.   I don't know. I guess not never.

HEWLETT.   You tellin' me you don't like it. All them people lookin' up at you, admirin' you. You don't get a chill up there? Standin' up there on that stage with all that applause fallin' down around you like warm summer rain.

ANN.   Yeah, I like it, I guess.

HEWLETT.   And wearin' that gown Sarah made for you. You look so pretty in that gown Annie. So, so pretty. Me and all those people out there, we want you to be our queen. We see you and we want to believe that you are our queen. So when they go back to them houses, they can wear them butler coats and footmen uniforms and handmaid outfits and dream. Dream of the lives they could live and the roles they could play if they only had a part. If there was only a place and a way for them to do it. But you, you have the chance and you don't want to do it.

ANN.   It's not that I don't want to do it. I just don't like that part. It just don't make no sense.

HEWLETT.   Annie, you're not tellin' me the truth.

23

ANN. Not tellin' the truth? What truth am I suppose to be tellin'? Ain't no truth in there for me.

HEWLETT. Yes there is. Only you in here bitin' when you otherwise wouldn't even be barkin'. This Ann, she ain't no different from Lady Ann. When that codfish aristocracy you house-maid for, does you wrong, do you holler? Do you throw up your hands with your apron clutched up in 'em and fling it down on the floor and tell 'em you ain't moppin' and dustin' and scrubbin' no more? That you are through sewin' up old clothes, washin' windows and cookin' up codfish to look like a rich man's dinner? Do you? No, you don't. 'Cause you know, you got to take it easy. You right to be mad, but you got to put a lid on that pot. You got to steam it down, 'til it gets to be a taste you can swallow. Lady Ann, she's in that king's kingdom, just like you in that man's house.

ANN. But he kills the woman's husband and her father.

HEWLETT. It's a play, Annie. You have to pretend.

ANN. Pretend? I don't know how to pretend. I don't have a husband. I don't know who my father is, nor my mother. There's just me. Every colored child come into this world is in a little basket on somebody's door step. And if she's a little girl, when she gets older where she starts lookin' like a woman, there is always some King Richard who wants to lie with her. And like it say in that play, they'll have us, but they won't keep us long. And the little baskets keep fillin' up with babies goin' from doorstep to doorstep to doorstep. Pretend? There ain't no pretendin' to that. How can I pretend?

HEWLETT. Then damn it Annie, if you can't do it, then kill it. Act one, scene two. Take up the sword and just bleed our dreams all over the floor. Make me the slave dealer and the people breeder and that hairy chest, just breathin' and heavin' and humpin' all over your body. Pick a spot on my lung. Lunge me with the knife and listen to the air suck out. Go ahead, kill it.

ANN. "Arise, dissembler! Though I wish thy death/ I will not be thy executioner."

HEWLETT. "Then bid me kill myself, and I will do it."

ANN. "I have all ready."

HEWLETT. "That was in thy rage:/ Speak it again, and even with the word,/ This hand, which for thy love did kill thy love,/ Shall for thy love kill a far truer love."

ANN. "I would I knew thy heart."

HEWLETT. "Tis figur'd in my tongue."

ANN. "I fear me both are false."

HEWLETT. "Then never man was true."

ANN. "Well, well, put up your sword."

HEWLETT. "Say, then, my peace is made."

ANN. "That shalt thou know hereafter."

HEWLETT. "But shall I live in hope?"

ANN. "All men, I hope, live so."

HEWLETT. "Vouchsafe to wear this ring."

ANN. "To take is not to give."

HEWLETT. "Look, how this ring encompasseth thy finger,/ Even so thy breast encloseth my poor heart;/ Wear both of them, for both of them are thine./ And if thy poor devoted suppliant may/ But beg one favor at thy gracious hand,/ Thou dost confirm his happiness for ever."

ANN. If my poor devoted suppliant did take my love, so he could be my love. And if that love be truer, if a ring on this finger can stop our dreams from bleeding on the floor. If I am to make you, the hairy chest that humps and heaves and breathes all over my body; then you already have my favors as you have my gracious hand.

HEWLETT. Annie, what is that? That's not the next line.

ANN. It's not?

HEWLETT. No it's not.

ANN. If I were Lady Ann, it would be the next line. I said it, didn't I? And what do you have to say?

HEWLETT. About what?

ANN. About what I said.

HEWLETT. Annie, it's not in the play. We're suppose to talk about what's in the play.

ANN. You mean to tell me that the only thing we have to talk about is in this play?

HEWLETT. Well, yes. That's what we doing here. We're rehearsing a play.

ANN.   No, that's what you doin' Jimmy. If that's all we got
to talk about, than talk to ya'self. This ain't no Lady Ann, this
Ann. This is me. *(Ann exits.)*
HEWLETT.   Annie, wait. Where're you goin'? Annie, come
back. Annie!

Scene 6

BROWN.   What exactly are ya doin' Constable-man?
THE CONSTABLE.   If you haven't noticed, I'm nailin' up a
sign. When I'm finished, you oughta be readin' it. You can
read, can't you.
BROWN.   What is all a this?
THE CONSTABLE.   The fire chief, he must 'a warned ya.
BROWN.   I ain't seen no fire chief.
THE CONSTABLE.   Well, maybe you was out when he
inspected this dump. Anyway, this place is a fire hazard. Too
many seats, not enough exits. And besides, it's disorderly. I've
had ya friend here, in my custody more than once. You'll
have to do your little plays somewheres else.
BROWN.   You needs all them posters to tell us that?
THE CONSTABLE.   No. These little leaflets are for the African Grove.
BROWN.   Not the African Grove.
THE CONSTABLE.   Sure, why not the African Grove. Your
nightly sarabands are too loud. Neighbors are complainin' you
keeping them up all night. You can thank your little friend
there for some a that too. Him and that drum a his. Here,
have one.
BROWN.   Ya love ya work, don't ya Constable-man.
THE CONSTABLE.   I do, Brownie, I do. Now, you two had
best be watchin' yourself, you hear me. 'Cause I'm keepin' a
sharp lookout on you. *(Exit the Constable.)*
PAPA SHAKESPEARE.   Look at dat one. He not just doin'
he duty. Him all smiles and so. *(Enter Hewlett.)*
HEWLETT.   Billy. Shakespeare. Have you seen Annie?
PAPA SHAKESPEARE.   No, we don't see she.

HEWLETT. I got to find her.

BROWN. Jimmy. You better read this.

HEWLETT. "This Grove is closed 'til further notice." Hey Billy, Papa-doctor, it's not the end of the world. Sometimes a bad thing has a way a comin' the good way 'round.

PAPA SHAKESPEARE. Good? What good be 'dere in dat?

HEWLETT. Now that people got nowheres to go, where they goin'? Rum shops like Douglas Club, Ike Hines, Johnny Johnson's?

PAPA SHAKESPEARE. They call demselves, tea garden clubs now.

HEWLETT. They rum shops, for Negroes to do nothin' but drink toddies and talk nonsense. Listen, lots a coloreds up here got good jobs. Boxers, jockeys. Remember, even I made some money recitin' and singin'. Negros comin' up here from the plantations and the cotton fields, they be tired a bein' in the woods. They wants to see the city. And they all don't want to go to no tea-garden club. Don't you see, the African Grove is closed, but now they can all come to see the African Theatre.

PAPA SHAKESPEARE. Long as they don't raise too much noise.

BROWN. You better read this one too, Jimmy.

HEWLETT. "Due to ... civil discord this theatre is closed." Discord? Discord? It's the partition. The partition. That goddamn partition. Puttin' the white people in the back. That's the nail that puts this paper up on the door. You went too far, Billy.

BROWN. You was thinkin' it was a good idea at the time. Ya didn't mind the white folks watchin' ya act, 'til now. And where else was they goin' to sit? They can't mix. They can't sit up front. They don't come here week after week the way the colored people do. Only reason they come a-tall, 'cause there's a partition for them to sit behind. They silly people and they love novelty.

HEWLETT. Novelty? Love novelty? It's no novelty to me. I don't care 'bout your partitions and your novelty. What'll I do with your novelty, now? Here. They serve notice on your novelty.

PAPA SHAKESPEARE. Jimmy. Billy. How you talk? Can ya see for lookin'? African Grove close up and same day, African Theatre got lock on de door. They all tie up. They puttin' they mark on we. Like conjure man sprinklin' brick dust and Johnny root 'cross ya road. More doin' here than talk and stories. Ya make people think big and want thing. Dem 'fraid a dat, ya know.

HEWLETT. Yes. Yes. Yes, doctor. *Richard the Third,* that's what it is. *Richard the Third* and Junius Brutus Booth. That's why the African Grove is closed and the African Theatre shut down.

BROWN. What Jimmy? What?

HEWLETT. Saturday night. This Saturday night. Saturday comin' the new Park Theatre opens with a Shakespearean play. Oh, it's supposed to be a grand affair. And for this great occasion they've got themselves a fine English star. A famous actor. A renowned mimic named Booth. And the play he's playin' in is the *Tragedy of King Richard the Third.*

PAPA SHAKESPEARE. Same as we.

BROWN. Ah, I see.

HEWLETT. How can his Richard be serious with the same words coming out a my mouth? With a black man 'cross town playin' his white king.

PAPA SHAKESPEARE. They don't want two Richards, they must have only one.

BROWN. I see.... Now Jimmy don't fear me now, but listen. This ain't the only place we can have a play. They other places where we can have a play.

HEWLETT. Where?

BROWN. Down the road, where you work, in the City Hotel, they got big ballroom, na so?

HEWLETT. They got two.

BROWN. They hire them out to a Negro?

HEWLETT. If that Negro got money.

BROWN. Then we doin' our Richard Three in one 'a them.

HEWLETT. But Billy, the City Hotel is right next door to the Park Theatre.

BROWN. Yes Jimmy, I know.

PAPA SHAKESPEARE. Ah yes.

Scene 7

SARAH.   You hear them men's talkin' Annie? They gettin'
ready to mix us up in some mess and they ain't even ask us.
Don't even want to know what we think. Supposin' old Van
Dam was to find I was spendin' my nights locked up in some
jail house somewheres. Why, I'd lose my job. How, what's the
matter with you, Annie? You lookin' so low. You havin'
troubles with Jimmy?
ANN.   I don't know what it is I got with Jimmy. I don't understand him. I tell him it don't make no sense to me and
he just wavin' his arm for me to go on and do it anyway.
"Trust me," he say. He wants to teach me everything, but he
don't want 'a teach me that. He don't want to teach me how
to trust him. It's mean, Sarah. It's mean. He put words in my
mouth, half the time I can hardly even say. And I have to say
'em so fast and they go through my mind so quick, it makes
me dizzy. Fixes my arms and my body all kinds a which 'a
ways, like I was a broom or a doll or somethin'. And I try
Sarah, I do. I try to make them Rs rounder and them Ss hiss
and them Ps and Bs pop and pound like he tell me to. But
I just don't feel it. I don't. It isn't me.
SARAH.   Well now, girl. It seems to me, like half ya troubles
come from you havin' so much willingness to learn.
ANN.   Say what?
SARAH.   You heard me. Wax ain't close up ya ears. You the
one followin' up behind that man.
ANN.   Who's followin' up behind who?
SARAH.   You. That's who. Battin' your eyelashes over every
little never-nothin' he say. Get on out from here, girl. You
know, I know. You just love that fancy talkin' men, that's all.
ANN.   It makes me mad, Sarah. Makes me mad.
SARAH.   And he knows it too. Knows you crazy 'bout him.
ANN.   I'm not gonna do it.
SARAH.   Well, all I got to say is, in my last life, I wasn't
nothin' but a 'ole slave. And I tell ya one thing, I had to

have me a master, is true. But I made up my mind early, there wasn't gone be but one a them. Nothin' or nobody was gone control me, lessin' I could help it. Specially no man....
Annie, what is that you say you not gone do?

ANN.   I'm not gonna be in this play.

SARAH.   You not gonna be in the play? What you mean, you not gonna be in the play?

ANN.   There's not gonna be no Lady Ann. If he wants to woo somebody, let him woo the wind. Let him talk his sweet nothin's to shadows and air. I'm not gonna be there.

SARAH.   But Annie, now think. You got to do the show, now. What 'bout all them people comin' up from down the Battery? Takin' the ferry from out Rockaway. Folks comin' down from way up Greenwich Village, have to walk back through the woods in the dark. Gettin' all dressed up. Fellas in their white pantaloons with the red ribbon and the bunch a pinch-beck seal 'round their coat collar. The ladies in their linen dresses and leghorn hats. Kid slippers and reticule on they arm. Shoot, girl, them people got to have someplace where they can gather, gossip, tell stories and whatever. Now the African Grove closed, ain't nowhere else to go. Oh, you got to do the play, honey.

ANN.   Don't sway me that way, Sarah. I feel this thing too deep.

SARAH.   Oh knowledge is sufferin', it's painful Annie, we all know that from birth. But what ya goin' do? Leave off from here, 'cause ya pride?

ANN.   Where do you see any pride in me? I hardly know my own mind, whereas I'm thinkin' a this man all the time. Seein' his face, hearin' his voice. Smellin' him. Where's the pride? My pride's already punishin' me.

SARAH.   O' baby, baby, don't wear ya burdens so loud.

ANN.   I can't help it.

SARAH.   Put some softness 'round you, sweetheart. Don't waste ya young world away, pinin' so.

ANN.   I can't help it, Sarah, I can't. It's what I need, what hurts me. I want some firmness in this hand a mine. Want 'a feel sweat from a skin I can depend on. I want somebody with me in this life. I'm goin' hurt 'til I get it. I'm not doin' no play actin' ...

SARAH.   No, Annie, no.

ANN.   I'm not gonna do it. I'm not.

BLACKOUT

ACT TWO

Scene 1

THE GRAND BALLROOM OF THE CITY HOTEL

PAPA SHAKESPEARE.   In the Islands, where I come from, there is still slavery there. My master 'dere he call me Shakespeare so to mock me, 'cause I don't speak the way he do. He laugh. He say me brow be wrinkled so, to mark me hard for thinkin'. But I say, this man, he no wise. He no hear me thinkin' in me own way. He don't see the one he name Shakespeare. He don't see, but I remember. I remember the forest and all de rivers that come down to the lagoon. And from among the mangroves and all along the seaside, I can hear them people talkin'. And man like my master come and take 'em away on ship and make 'em slaves. But still, I hear them. Even now, I hear them. They mouths and they tongues, they go knockin' and rollin'. They go ... *(Clucking and clicking sounds.)* I hear them. They're in my head and will stay there so long as I remember. Where I come from, the book is a living man. And we must read from what he say. It more hard for a man to lie, than a book. 'Cause we see him everyday and we know what he does and see where he goes. Everywhere them boys, they come from far. From Barbados, St. Lucia, Tortola, John's Island. From all 'round. And what they hear when they come to the towns, they must listen to the one, who can tell them what the white man is saying. This one, who tell 'em so, he name Griot. I say, Griot. Sometime, when This Man over here, wish to speak to That Man over 'dere. Each one speaks to the Griot and the Griot tells the one what the other is saying. Like so. This Man say: "Griot, ask that low, snake like dog, why is he chasing my wife."

32

And the Griot, he say to That Man: "That Man. This Man, he say, he knows your love for him is great, but must you love his wife so greatly as well?"

And That Man say: "Griot, tell This Man, that only a fool could love so ugly a fish face woman as his wife."

So the Griot say: "This Man. That Man he say he only loves your beautiful wife out of his great love and respect for you."

This is the way the Griot works. This is what he does. If Shakespeare was a black man, he would be a Griot. So, I say, though my master mock me, it be no mock to me. *(Enter Sarah.)* Oh Sarah. How de body, Sarah?

SARAH.   My body? My body is fine, Shakespeare.

PAPA SHAKESPEARE.   What you got 'dere Sarah? What ya doin' wit all dem bundles so?

SARAH.   This bundle? The costume stuff is in this bundle. I lug this thing all the way uptown tryin' not to drag 'em 'cross these filthy streets. Lord, this is one slack place, this New York City. The stage coach goin' to Greenwich Village splatter mud on me. The boy carryin' he bucket from the corner pump, splash water on me and I almost trap over the hog eatin' trash in the street.

PAPA SHAKESPEARE.   What you got in 'dat bundle, you so careful so?

SARAH.   I got me some tinsel to trim the drapery. And some new leggins for Jimmy. How you like these?

PAPA SHAKESPEARE.   Oh, Jimmy gonna look plenty nice in them.

SARAH.   Then there's these rags and tatters to patch up things. Here's a brand new bonnet for Annie.

PAPA SHAKESPEARE.   Oh, Annie gonna look too nice on that topper.

SARAH.   And how 'bout this hand-me-down, Sunday-go-to-meetin', pigeon-tailed coat for Mr. Catesby.

PAPA SHAKESPEARE.   Ah Sarah, that's too nice. What for you go and do a thing like this, huh Sarah?

SARAH.   Well, you was lookin' kinda shabby Shakespeare, so I say to myself, being that this is our big night and all, I was gonna see if I could rummage up a new coat for the fellow, Catesby.

PAPA SHAKESPEARE.   Oh look at me now. Now I can run 'round on me errands lookin' like I suppose to. *(Sarah applauds as Shakespeare models his formal coat.)* Thank you, thank you, thank you. Oh Sarah, I say, it be like the Bible say, "You reap what you sow." They try to shut us down, 'cause the Constable-man say for danger from fire and civil dis code. And here we are now, performin' the same show as he. And now, they gonna be chewin' the soup they done swallow.

SARAH.   Yes, I got to give it to your boy, Billy. That Negro got him a lot a nerve. First he build a Negro theatre and put the white folks in the back. And it ain't two nights since the Constable-man hisself come and shut us down. And what Billy Brown do? Didn't he hire the grand ballroom of the City Hotel ...

PAPA SHAKESPEARE.   ... Right next door to the man's theatre.

SARAH.   I never thought I would ever see nothin' like that before. Colored man talkin' back to a white man. Shute, where I come from you be listenin' to whip lash and chewin' dry bone, behind that kinda back talk. Oh, I almost forgot. I got us these merino curtins from the grand ballroom of the hotel here, for King Richard's new robe.

PAPA SHAKESPEARE.   From this grand ballroom of this self-same hotel?

SARAH.   Yes, this grand ballroom of this self-same City Hotel. You want to know how I got 'em?

PAPA SHAKESPEARE.   Yes. I want to know how you get them draper off the wall without nobody seein' ya do so.

SARAH.   I didn't steal 'em. I ain't never stole nothin' in my life. Mrs. Van Dam got 'em for me.

PAPA SHAKESPEARE.   Mrs. Van Dam?

SARAH.   Yes. The woman gone and sneak out her house to come see me play the Queen, honey. She come all the way up from Bowling Green by herself. Try to hide herself back 'dere in the back. In the dark.

PAPA SHAKESPEARE.   So that the reason you walk away

from me when I'm talkin' to you and you go on and leave the stage. For go talkin' to that man.

SARAH.   That wasn't no man. That was Mrs. Van Dam. She had on this here, long coat, as hot as it was, and it was dragin' all along the floor. She wearin' this great, tall stovepipe hat, come down nearly coverin' her eyes. So I look. I thought that was her. Now, her hat is so big, that this little man behind her, couldn't hardly see. He tellin' her, "Mr. will you remove your hat?" Man tryin' to take her hat, little old Van Dam holdin' it down on her head. She so nervous, poor thing, she don't know what to do. That's when you say to me.... Now, what's that you say to me again?

PAPA SHAKESPEARE.   "Madam, his Majesty doth call for you."

SARAH.   That's right. Well, my majesty musta called, 'cause I gone and left the stage to go down there to see if that was little old Van Dam. I asked her, I said Mrs. Van Dam, what are you doin' here? She say, "I come to see you play the Queen, Sarah." I told her, I said, well Mrs. Van Dam this is no place for you to be all by yourself. And you know what she said to me? She said, "Oh Sarah, I'm so sorry. I never knew you. You live in my house and all day long you listen to my worries. I tell you all my confidences, just because you won't talk back. And I don't know a thing about you." She said, "Sarah, what can I do for you? Anything." So I told her, I said if I could have some material like the curtains hanging over the ballroom window at the City Hotel, I could make a new robe for King Richard. She refuse to leave, so I had to let her stay. So I sat her right down front. Lord, that was some sight to see. Little old Van Dam sittin' there in a sea a black faces. She so silly, she think nobody can see there's a woman in them men's clothes. I get back to the house that night and there's Mrs. Van Dam in the sittin' room with the needles and the thread and the scissors and the City Hotel's grand ballroom curtains spread out on the sittin' room floor. She swear, she say she's comin' here tonight to see me play the Queen. Gonna sneak out dressed like a man again. I sure hope she don't get in no trouble.

PAPA SHAKESPEARE. I can see you there now. The two of ya. Mrs. Van Dam and you Sarah. You the only one got one name. They don't call ya last name.

SARAH. Last name? I ain't got no last name. Every last name I ever had, belong to somebody else. I suppose right now, my last name would be Van Dam. Sarah Van Dam, can you imagine? Lord, Papa Shakespeare, ownin' people must do some strange things to you spiritually. I miss Georgia, that's one pretty land. But I'm glad I'm free. And now, the old girl is comin' again to see me be a Queen in a play.

PAPA SHAKESPEARE. And you know, you do that Queen a England part good, Sarah.

SARAH. Do you really think so, Shakespeare?

PAPA SHAKESPEARE. Oh yes. I like best the part where I hear you sayin', "... too long have I borne/ Your unbraidings and bitter scoffs/ of those taunts I have oft endur'd/ I had rather be a country servant-maid/ Than a grear queen in this condition/ To be baited and scor'd so." Somethin' goin right through me, when you sayin' that part, Sarah.

SARAH. You know, you look good in that coat, Shakespeare.

PAPA SHAKESPEARE. No, I don't Sarah. Me no have fun like you do play actin' the Queen Elizabeth, while me hammy actin' at Catesby. Tiresome little man, always runnin' this way and so.

SARAH. What part would you rather play?

PAPA SHAKESPEARE. Jimmy say, I go do more than Catesby now. Also King Henry's ghost. He say in Act One, I go be a soldier, Sir Brakenbury. But I don't see nobody in 'dere who I can be. I rather have me own play.

SARAH. And if you had your own play, Shakespeare, what kind of hero would you be in it?

PAPA SHAKESPEARE. I would be a character who was very big. As tall as ten palm trees put together. A body like iron. As swift as lightin'. When I turn 'round, everything move and sway so. It be like Jimmy say, like Gulliver among the Lilliputians. In the mornin', when I'm going down to the sea-side, where I step is lagoons filled with fresh water. I carry a big machete to cut down the cane. Make me blood sacrifice a top a dem wild green hills. I got all kinds a roots to make the people's body well. And every day I'm throwin' the bones to see how they lay. To see the future. And what I see, I see all the people. And de body well. *(Sarah puts the King's robe around Papa Shakespeare.)*

SARAH.   You look real good in that robe, Shakespeare.

PAPA SHAKESPEARE.   Thank you Sarah. *(Enter Hewlett.)*

HEWLETT.   Sarah. Shakespeare. Where's Annie?

SARAH.   Where's Annie? We don't know where Annie is. What, you don't know how to find her? It's a wonder you even know she gone.

HEWLETT.   Gone? Where she gone to?

SARAH.   Gone, Jimmy, she just gone. It don't matter to you where she gone to, 'cause it ain't a place where you welcome. She gone. She not comin' back. She not gonna be in this play. You got to play ya King Richard all by yourself.

PAPA SHAKESPEARE.   What's the matter with Annie?

SARAH.   Annie don't like that part, she and Jimmy be doin' together, ya know.

HEWLETT.   Yes but Sarah, it's only a story in a play.

SARAH.   It ain't just a story to Annie. It's her feelin's. Annie's feelin's is what I'm talking about. You hurt that girl, Jimmy and she loves you.

HEWLETT.   Sarah, I didn't mean no harm.

SARAH.   Still harm is done. You don't know where to find her. Treatin' her like that after all she do to try and help you with this theatre. She don't hardly have no time to herself, the way the white folks be workin' her. But she do it anyway. Why? For you. You ain't even much know. She didn't want to do no play-actin' in the beginnin'. She only doin' it, 'cause that's what you want.

HEWLETT.   Sarah, we have to find her. Find her for me. Please Sarah. Please.

SARAH.   I'll go look for her. I'll try to find her. But you the one got to say somethin' to her.

HEWLETT.   Shakespeare, you've got the robe. I've been looking for it everywhere.

PAPA SHAKESPEARE.   How I look Jimmy. It's a brand new

robe. Sarah been up the whole night makin' it into life.

HEWLETT.   And what are you doing with it on? Take it off. Give it to me.

SARAH.   Jimmy!

PAPA SHAKESPEARE.   Ya know Jimmy, back home how the cock crow? You don't hear 'em crow down 'dere like 'e do na ya. It make a man so he don't know what time to get up in the mornin'. Ya soundin' like some kinda a cane boss, Jimmy. Words poppin' and crackin' off ya tongue like a whip. Here, take ya robe. I'm goin' on behind Sarah. Don't want no more cane raisin 'round near me now. *(Exit Sarah and Papa Shakespeare.)*

Scene 2

BROWN.   Annie, Annie, Annie, why ya so stubborn?

ANN.   No.

BROWN.   But Annie, ya got to come back.

ANN.   No.

BROWN.   Listen Annie. Listen to me.

ANN.   No.

BROWN.   It's the best scene in the whole play. That's what the people come to see. Not just Jimmy, but you too, Annie. And Jimmy knows it. That's why he send all us 'round looking everywhere to find ya. Beggin' ya. Annie, please come back.

ANN.   Billy Brown, you like a muslin curtain hanging front 'a the window, light shinin' right through you. Jimmy ain't send you. Jimmy don't even know you here. You ain't talkin' 'bout Jimmy, you talkin' 'bout ya self.

BROWN.   No Annie, no. Believe me. It's Jimmy. It's Jimmy that wants you back. I mean, we all want you back.

ANN.   Billy, I see you. You ain't foolin' nobody. We heard you. Me and Sarah both. We heard what you'll fixin' to do. Onliest thing you need us for, is to mix us up in it. Tell the truth.

BROWN.   We can't let them people have they way with us

and not do nothin' 'bout it.

ANN.   Yes they do have their way with us and we can't do nothin' 'bout it. But that's the way it is with you Billy. You always want to confront. Why? Why can't you just pay them people no mind?

BROWN.   Pay them people no mind? I only wish. Is that how you see me, Annie? Always want to confront and use people. That all you see me for?

ANN.   No, 'course not. I ain't sayin' anything is wrong with you, the way you are. I just don't know what I'm gonna do for my own self.

BROWN.   I hate seein' ya so sour, Annie. I guess you know best how to do for ya'self. Me only sayin', I wish you would join us in this ting, ya know.

ANN.   I don't know, Billy. I don't know.

BROWN.   What if I get Jimmy. He'll tell ya hisself how he's sorry. How 'bout that. That be okay?

ANN.   Don't play with me Billy, I'm not nobody's little girl.

BROWN.   You crazy 'bout you some Jimmy, ain't you girl?

ANN.   No more crazy than I am for toothache and body lice.

BROWN.   Why?

ANN.   Why? Why what?

BROWN.   Why Jimmy?

ANN.   Why Jimmy? I don't know. Why does a rooster crow? Why wool hat make ya head itch? What you sayin' to me Billy? Why you ask me that? Are you.... Oh Billy. Oh no Billy. Billy, you know what makes me so mad? What hurts me? Times when Jimmy don't even know I'm on this earth. And now here you come.

BROWN.   You don't have to say nothin'.

ANN.   Why you wait 'til now? You couldn't talk before?

BROWN.   You comin' back with us or no?

ANN.   I'm sorry Billy. I didn't see before. I see it now. I do. I don't know what to say. I'm sorry.

BROWN.   You with us in this 'ting or no?

ANN.   I don't know, Billy. If you do this thing tonight, there ain't gonna be no African Theatre after that. So why you doin' it?

BROWN.   When I was a boy back down in the Islands, on the plantation, workin' in the cane fields. I seein' the overseer readin' and writin' in that book he carry 'round everyday. And I wonderin' to myself, what them marks he makin' on that paper. And I watch that white man and I watch him. After while, he see me lookin' so, he show me. I didn't know what them marks on that paper was. So he teach me. Papa Shakespeare, he was a young man then, but he knew things. Things he learned as a boy in Africa. He was the only one among us, who could point out into the sea to where Africa was. When some were sick, he knew the herbs to make 'em well. When one of us died or the women had baby or when we had to name the children, he knew what to do. While in the day, that overseer teach me how to read what it say in he book. Night time come, the old Papa-Doctor, he teach us the way thing be. It ain't enough for you to say what you want when people can tell you, how you can say 'em, and when you can say 'em, and where. Now, are you with us in this 'ting or no?

Scene 3

HEWLETT.   Now is the hour of our discontent
Made glorious summer by this sun of York
And all the clouds that lowered over our house
In the deep bosom of the ocean buried ...
Where was that? Where was it? Saratoga, that was it. Saratoga, New York. In the ballroom of the United States Hotel. "James Hewlett, vocalist and Shakespeare's proud representative will now give an entertainment of dramatic exhibition and song." The room is very cold and still. The people a sea of gray expressionless faces, covering me with waves of coughing and shifting and squinting their eyes as if they would drown me. "He's going to do Hamlet! He's going to do Hamlet" some old powder face shouts.... "To be or not to be, that is the question".... My mouth was like it was full of stones, and with

every word I spoke a stone fell to the floor. I couldn't hear myself speak. The very air itself seemed like it didn't want to come into me.... "Whether 'tis nobler in the mind to suffer the slings and arrows of outrageous fortune".... And then there came the laughter. Pushed, forced out, coming at me, chasing me, running me down with laughter. But it was good somehow, because you see with every laugh there grew a face. And so I smiled. Not a lot, but just a little, small smile.... "Or to take up arms against a sea of troubles/ And by opposing end them." And then one of the faces stood up in his chair, "Did you say by opossum end them?" No, no. I said, "by opposing end them." Then that laughing face, so clear and so sure, told me what they all wanted me to do. They wanted me to sing. To sing the song, "opossum up a gum tree." Do you know how it goes? Shall I sing it for you? Sing it or else?
Opossum up a gum tree/ Creepy slow
Raccoon in de holluw/ Down below
Pull opossum by he long tail/ Down he go
Raccoon back in hollow/ Nigga down below
Pull opposum by him long tail/ Raccoon let 'em go
Jiinkum, jankim, mymum/ Hollar to the moon
Oh de cunning nigger/ Oh de poor raccoon
(Enter Brown and Papa Shakespeare.)
BROWN. Jimmy!
HEWLETT. Here he is. Enter Mr. William Henry Brown our great proprietor "mise en scene" who makes Shakespeare into his great Negro revolt.
BROWN. What is the matter with you Jimmy?
HEWLETT. What's the matter with me? What, you don't see? You don't see all those people out there? You don't see the Constable and his watchmen, all come to see the African Richard?
BROWN. What is this you talkin' 'bout Jimmy?
HEWLETT. I'm talking about you Billy. You and how you killin' the African Theatre.
BROWN. Me? Killin' the African Theatre?
HEWLETT. Killin' it. Breathing death on it like a plague. You knew damn well they was gonna shut us down. You knew

it all along. I think it was what you wanted from the first.

BROWN.   Many time as we been shut down before, this is some great mystery and tragedy to you? You ain't foolin' nobody Jimmy. Ya just want a keep on play-actin' ya Shakespeare.

HEWLETT.   My play-actin' Shakespeare got you far enough to act out your great Negro revolt. How come you the one get to say what we all should know? What we all should think. What we all should do. What you gonna do? Change the world with a play?

BROWN.   Listen you complainin' now. How what's the matter? This ain't what you want? You on the same street, in the same play. And nothin' ain't change for you? It ain't change, has it. You a nigger up on Mercer Street. You a nigger down here.

HEWLETT.   We don't have to do this. We don't have to do it.

BROWN.   It's already done. Been done. Been done long time now.

HEWLETT.   Why you doin' this to me?

BROWN.   To you?

HEWLETT.   Yes to me. Why are you doin' this to me?

BROWN.   What people will see tonight is the whole story. They gonna know tonight what you know now. That we alone in this world with nobody but ourselves to turn loose on. That you and ya shadow make two and there's little body else to take up ya cause. Play-actin'. What do you get for your play-actin' Jimmy?

HEWLETT.   I get to be loved and to be accepted. To be openly admired. To feel myself, to be full of myself. To breath air and give it back again. To make myself as if I were clay. To press my fingers against me and give me shape. The make-up, the costumes, the robe. It's all glass that I know how to polish and make clear. So that any man can see that I am any man. You talk with such a twisted tongue Billy. This isn't your African Theatre. It's ours. And with all a this little bit a freedom we got here Billy, where's mine? Where the hell is mine? Where?

BROWN. You have it. It's there in your head and here in your heart and in your hands. You got a mouth, it got voice. You don't need no crowd clappin' for you to know so. Tonight they gonna be more theatre out on them cobble stones, than in here lookin' at ya Black Richard. Them what can't read, can see. And when the Constable-man come, them what don't know, gonna understand. Ya see, our Black Richard is a hit, ya know. We tellin' everybody, that our ways, our ideas, our beliefs be just as good as theirs. These ain't no imitations. It's us. We. You say that this is our African Theatre. Then you are "our" Black Richard. What you wear, the way you speak, what you do, how you feel. This is what we want to see and hear. You, are what we want. Gives us imitations and we'll be throwin' apple cores and ginger cakes at you ourselves. Tonight Jimmy, the air you be breathin' gonna be full a sweat, drippin' down ya chest and tricklin' down back ya neck. Thick air Jimmy, what you can bite with ya teeth and weave 'round in ya hands. Forgets what them fancy-full people think, them high-blowin' elitists, and say ya Shakespeare like ya want. "Now is de winter of our discontentment made de glorious summer by dis son a New York." They gonna love it Jimmy. They gonna love it.

PAPA SHAKESPEARE. Jimmy, Annie she is just outside.

HEWLETT. Annie?

PAPA SHAKESPEARE. She's just there, outside. She says, she can't come back unless she has a reason. Otherwise she is just throwin' away her pride. I told her, I said, don't worry, Jimmy will apologize to you. She shook her head. She said, "no." She wouldn't believe me. So, I told her you told me so ya'self. You said, "Go find her Papa Shakespeare and bring her back so I can apologize to her." Don't fuss, say. She is comin' now. *(Enter Ann.)* Come Annie, here's Jimmy. He wants to speak with you.... He is so glad to see you, that he is speechless just now.... He is gettin' ready to talk now.... Listen carefully, he is about to speak.

HEWLETT. Annie ...

PAPA SHAKESPEARE. You see. What did I tell you, now he's talkin'.

HEWLETT. Annie, why did you run off like that. You put the play at risk.

PAPA SHAKESPEARE. He say, he was very worried when you went away and he didn't know where you were.

ANN. The play? Put the play at risk? That's all you think about is that damn play. I'll show you a play, all right ...

PAPA SHAKESPEARE. She is sayin' Jimmy, how she admires so much how dedicated you are.

ANN. You don't give one red penny for nobody's feelin's ...

PAPA SHAKESPEARE. Your generosity of spirit.

ANN. You ain't the only one smart ...

PAPA SHAKESPEARE. Your wisdom.

ANN. You ain't the only one got to struggle ...

PAPA SHAKESPEARE. Your sacrifices.

ANN. You're selfish ...

PAPA SHAKESPEARE. That self-confidence you got.

ANN. Overbearing and arrogant.

PAPA SHAKESPEARE. Your patience and humility. She like all a them.

ANN. And further more, I'm not doin' no play. And if you think my bark is bigger than my bite, then you go ahead and just try to make me.

PAPA SHAKESPEARE. She say, maybe she'll play Lady Ann tonight. She's only just thinkin' about it, now. Why don't you say somethin' to her. Go on man, just clear ya throat and talk.

HEWLETT. Annie. Annie, what do you want me to say?

ANN. I didn't come back in here to hear you deliver no riddles.

PAPA SHAKESPEARE. He's tryin' to tell you he's sorry.

ANN. Well, tell him to tell it then.

PAPA SHAKESPEARE. She says you're beatin' 'round the bush.

HEWLETT. Look Annie, how was I suppose to know?

PAPA SHAKESPEARE. Ah, he didn't know. How's that? He would have talk with you before, but he just didn't know.

ANN. Tell him if he didn't have his head stuck way up in the clouds, he would know.

PAPA SHAKESPEARE. She says, next time you should think more clearly.

HEWLETT. All right, all right, all right. Annie I'm sorry.

ANN. Does he really expect me to believe that?

PAPA SHAKESPEARE. You goin' to have to talk a little more. You're not quite bringin' her 'round.

HEWLETT. She thinks I'm selfish. Ask her why she wasn't thinkin' of all those people come to see their African Richard. Ask her that.

PAPA SHAKESPEARE. He says, that it's not true that he's a selfish man. He cares for people very much and you more so than others.

ANN. That's not what he said.

PAPA SHAKESPEARE. Yes he did. I hear him plainly. He is tellin' you, he would tell you so hisself, but him pride get in the way. No so Jimmy?

HEWLETT. Tell her, I didn't mean to hurt her.

PAPA SHAKESPEARE. Tell her so, ya'self.

HEWLETT. I didn't mean to hurt you, Annie. I'm sorry.

PAPA SHAKESPEARE. He says that all his struggles would be too hard to bear without you. Look at his eyes, listen to what he is sayin'. He loves you.

ANN. Jimmy Hewlett, in love with who?

PAPA SHAKESPEARE. She say, she always hoped you did.

ANN. Is that true Jimmy? What you have to say?

PAPA SHAKESPEARE. He say, stop talkin', you embrassin' him. Come give him a hug. (*Hewlett and Ann embrace.*) Ah, it be so. (*Enter Sarah.*)

SARAH. Billy. Billy, a man. A white man is here to see you.

BROWN. A white man?

SARAH. Yes, he say he run the Park Theatre.

HEWLETT. It's Price. Stephen Price.

SARAH. Yes, that's the name, Price. He's here. He's standin' over by the door, waitin' to come in.

BROWN. Then show 'em in, Sarah. (*Sarah goes off and ushers Price in.*)

PRICE. Mr. William Henry Brown, I presume?

BROWN. Yes sir, that's me, Billy Brown.

PRICE.   My name is Price. Stephen Price. I'm the manager of the Park Theatre.

BROWN.   How do you do, sir.

PRICE.   I must congratulate you Brown, on your fine work with the African Company.

BROWN.   Why, thank you sir. But Jimmy here, is our real star.

PRICE.   James Hewlett. Who would have thought. It's been a long time, James. Not since the day George Cooke died.

HEWLETT.   Yes sir, it's been a long time.

PRICE.   I read your reviews. You've become a fine actor. Remarkably good diction and your pronunciations are quite good really. You certainly made good use of your employ with old George as his man servant and dresser.

HEWLETT.   That's very kind of you Mr. Price.

PRICE.   Nonsense, it's the truth. I understand you're a waiter in this Hotel.

HEWLETT.   Yes sir. I am a waiter here.

PRICE.   The next time we supper here, we must remember to dine in your section. Mr. Brown, may I have a word?

BROWN.   Which word would you like, sir?

PRICE.   A word. A word with you. Mr. Brown, you have been fairly successful with your Richard. I don't suppose you do any other shows.

BROWN.   No, there's no other show, just now sir. People like our Richard just fine.

PRICE.   Well, you see, we change our shows regularly. Next door we have a very famous English actor who has come all the way from England to perform at the Park Theatre. I don't know if you've ever heard of him. His name is Booth. Junius Brutus Booth.

BROWN.   Brutus, sir? Like in Julius Caesar?

PRICE.   Yes, that's right, like in Julius Caesar. You see we have what we call an exclusive contract with Mr. Booth. That means that he performs at our theatre only if we promise to bring him a broad public. This opening is very important. We want to thank him for coming all the way over here, from England. The mayor will be there, the governor. Perhaps you've heard of James Fenimore Cooper or Washington Irving.

BROWN. Sounds very nice, sir.

PRICE. How many nights a week; do you play in your Mercer Street house?

BROWN. Six nights sir.

PRICE. Six? That many. That's a lot. And how many people do you get in there?

BROWN. That's hard to say, sir.

PRICE. Hard to say? The fire chief, who is my friend, tells me you squeeze three hundred in there. You broke the fire codes and the Constable had to come and shut you down. But I'll tell you what I'll do, Mr. Brown. Go back to your Mercer Street theatre and I'm prepared, right now to give you two hundred dollars a week, to buy out your houses from to-night, until our Richard closes.

BROWN. That would be most generous of you, sir. But we don't see how we can turn all those people away, for only two hundred dollars. As a businessman, I'm sure you understand, sir.

PRICE. You're a very shrewd fellow, Brown. I like that. All right, three hundred dollars. Three hundred dollars a week, that's my best offer. What do you say?

BROWN. Well sir, you see Mr. Price, when I come to New York, I was already grown. Too old to go to the colored free school here, but my arithmetic is not so bad. The people who come to the African Theatre, they are people who can't afford to go to your theatre. They only pay a quarter with us. And as you say sir, there are three hundred chairs and the people can come six nights a week. Three hundred dollar is not quite fair, sir.

PRICE. You drive a very hard bargain Brown. Three hundred and fifty.

BROWN. Forgive me sir, but I was thinkin' that four hundred dollar would be very fair.

PRICE. Look, don't play with me Brown. What do you expect me to do, guarantee your house. I wish I had four hundred a week guaranteed and a good holiday. Three seventy-five and that's the top.

BROWN. Thank you sir, thank you. That's most kind. You,

too, too nice sir. A very generous offer. Thank you, sir. Thank you very much.... But I'm afraid that we must keep our own Richard. You, of course are welcome. And for no charge sir.
PRICE.   I see. James, always nice to see you again. Ladies. It's in your hands now, Mr. Brown. The bird and the bush. And as my King Richard would say, I urge you to "Set down the corse." Good evening, gentlemen. *(Exit Price.)*
SARAH.   What does he mean, "set down the corse?"
HEWLETT.   The corse. He means the dead body of King Henry. It's from a line in the play, "Villains set down the corse; or by Saint Paul,/ I'll make a corse of him that disobeys"
PAPA SHAKESPEARE.   Three hundred seventy-five dollar is a lot a money, Billy. That man he fixin' to make trouble.
ANN.   Billy. Jimmy. What are we gonna do?
HEWLETT.   We gonna open the doors Annie, and let the people in. And like "our" King Richard would say. "Shine out, fair sun, 'til I have bought a glass, that I may see my shadow as I pass."
BROWN.   I come from cane field and gone to sea. Don't got no paper, say I'm a free man. So this sailorman and this captain, they shakin' they purse, bitin' they coin, fixin' to sell me to the slave dealerman for five hundred dollar. "Where this nigga come from," sailorman say. I don't want to tell him, I come from cane field boss. Captain say, "this nigga don't want to say where he come from, but he back strong." Slave dealerman say, "I don't care were he come from, long as he don't go to hell, before I'm through." But I cut cane and I know, it's too dear. Black woman dragin' cane and cuttin', children working in the fields, 'e too dear. On some farms they breed the people like dogs. They make the men be studs and the women be bitches. 'E too dear. Them steal away ya past and cut ya from ya future. Make ya blood into a purse to fill with gold and silver. But 'e too dear. Two hundred dollar, three hundred dollar, three-fifty, three-seventy five, four-hundred dollar, five. 'E too dear.

Scene 4

CONSTABLE.   Well sir, Mr. Price sir, did you manage to talk any sense into them?

PRICE.   No Constable, I'm afraid I did not.

CONSTABLE.   Oh no sir. They're not going to go through with it?

PRICE.   Yes Constable, I'm afraid they are.

CONSTABLE.   You want me and the boys to go shut 'em down now?

PRICE.   No, wait a few minutes. Let them get started. Wait until the curtain rises and that Hewlett boy is in the middle of his little speech and then I want you to go and pull him down from there. And don't just close it. I want them locked up.

CONSTABLE.   I don't know how long I can keep 'em sir. What law are they breakin'?

PRICE.   What law are they breaking? The law of nature, man. People must listen to generosity and not scoff at it. We are not slave masters, or slave catchers. These people are free. And the only reason they are is an invisible line called the thirty-sixth parallel and because politicans don't know what to do with them. But this is our world. We made it for ourselves. This isn't just any opening night, it's "the" opening night. The Mayor, the Governor, James Cooper, Irving, the Washington Hall bunch. All of them, every bloody one of them will come riding up in their carriages to witness this bloody catastrophe. Booth won't even speak to me. Imagine that. How do you like your "serious" Shakespeare hosting a circus outside and a farce next door. The arrogance of him, to put up his tent show next door to my theatre. Well, I offered him reasonable fees for a reasonable favor. I don't relish being made a fool of. Tonight the curtain falls on Mr. Brown's little sable pageant. And they'll swear before whatever God they swear, never, never, never to play Shakespeare again. Or by heaven, they will never see the light of day.

Scene 5

PAPA SHAKESPEARE.   So, de Constable-man he out 'dere.
He and all the constabulary, they come takin' up all a the
people's chair. Standin' back in de corner by de darkness.
Some is by de door, 'dere and others is 'round de back. They
all come to shut us down. They darin' us so. We say one
word a what my brother William say and they lock us up.
Now, you people come na ya to see the play. And some come
to see 'em not play. So, the African Theatre is now givin' two
stories for the price a one.

And now, all of de characters will become real. The black
Richard, the black Ann, the Queen Sarah, the black Rivers,
the black Catesby. All gonna breâth air and live as you do.
See 'em na ya, if he no so.

LADIES AND GENTLEMEN!
THE AFRICAN COMPANY PRESENTS!
THE TRAGEDY OF KING RICHARD THREE!
BY MY BROTHER WILLIAM SHAKESPEARE!
ACT ONE, SCENE ONE!

HEWLETT.   "Now is the winter of our discontent
Made glorious summer by this sun of York;
And all the clouds that lowered upon our house
In the deep bosom of the ocean buried.
Now are our brows bound with victorious wreaths,
Our bruised arms hung up for monuments,
Our stern alarms changed to merry meetings,
Our dreadful marches to delightful measures.
Grim-visaged war hath smoothed his wrinkled front,
And now, instead of mounting barbed steeds
To fright the souls of fearful adversaries;
He capers nimbly in a lady's chamber
To the lascivious pleasing of a lute.
But I, that am not shaped for sportive tricks

Nor made to court an amorous looking glass;
I, that am curtailed of this fair proportion,
Cheated of feature by dissembling nature,
Deformed, unfinished, sent before my time
Into this breathing world, scarce half made up,
And that so lamely and unfashionable
That dogs bark at me as I halt by them —
Why, I, in this weak piping time of peace
Have no delight to pass away the time,
Unless to see my shadow in the sun
And descent on mine own deformity
And therefore, since I cannot prove a lover
To entertain these fair well-spoken days,
I am determined to prove a villain
And hate the idle pleasures of these days.

CONSTABLE.   Hello! Hey you! Hey you there! Come down off a there!

HEWLETT.   "Plots have I laid, inductions dangerous,
By drunken prophecies, libels and schemes

CONSTABLE.   Did you hear me? I said come down from there! You're under arrest!

HEWLETT.   "To set my brother Clarence and the king
In deadly hate the one against the other;

CONSTABLE.   None a your play-actin' airs, it's into the black-hole with the lot of you.

HEWLETT.   "And if King Edward be as true and just
As I am subtle, false and treacherous,

CONSTABLE.   Stop it, I said! Did ya hear me? There'll be no more Shakespeare in here!

HEWLETT.   "This day should Clarence closely be mewed up

CONSTABLE.   All right, move along! Everybody out!

HEWLETT.   "About a prophecy which says that "G"
Of Edward's heirs ...

CONSTABLE.   This establishment is closed!

HEWLETT.   "... the murderer shall he.

CONSTABLE.   Violation of the fire code!

HEWLETT.   "Dive, thoughts down to soul;

CONSTABLE.   Civil disorder!
HEWLETT.   "... here Clarence comes!"
CONSTABLE.   And you're makin' too much noise!

Scene 6

THE ELDRIDGE STREET JAIL

There are three square pools of light representing three jail cells. Sarah and Ann are in one; Hewlett and Brown are in another; and between them, in the center square, is Papa Shakespeare in a cell to himself.

PAPA SHAKESPEARE.   Here I am lock up in this jail house again. And 'e so cramp up and dark in here.
SARAH.   I can't believe how they rush us in here, make me mess up my dress. Up there talkin' 'bout we break the law. Whose law we breaking, that's what I want 'a know. Papa Shakespeare, did they get ya drum?
PAPA SHAKESPEARE.   No Sarah, I got it hide under me coat. It's in here lock up in the jail cell with me.
SARAH.   O' thank the Lord for that Shakespeare. Well I guess old Van Dam gone have to waltz with somebody else, 'cause we not gone swear we ain't gone do no Shakespeare, is we Billy?
BROWN.   Sure we gone swear. Why not swear?
ANN.   I can't believe that's you talkin' Billy. You gone swear? Swear what? Swear us into silence?
BROWN.   We can't do no Shakespeare in here. Ya damn right we'll swear.
HEWLETT.   You swear then. 'Cause I ain't swearin' to nothin'.
ANN.   Me neither.
SARAH.   Nor me neither.
PAPA SHAKESPEARE.   We swear Billy, and then we go and

do it anyway, they gonna lock us up each and every time. Even before we get started, they gone stop us. We never have a chance. They will go make a law, say that we can't carry Shakespeare no more. How we gone swear?

BROWN.   How, what's the matter with all 'a you people? What, we got to do Shakespeare like his mouth the only mouth what speak? Cat have tongue too ya know. Taste just as good sayin' words comin' from one who knows who you are, than one who don't know ya a' tall.

ANN.   And where are these good tastin' words comin' from? What they gone be sayin'?

SARAH.   Yeah and who's gone be speakin' 'em? Tell me that.

BROWN.   Sarah. Do you see him down there? Do you see the Constable-man anywhere?

SARAH.   No, I don't see him. I don't see no Constable-man now.

BROWN.   Jimmy.

HEWLETT.   What do you want with me now, Billy?

BROWN.   Here Jimmy, have a look at this. *(Hewlett takes a manuscript and begins reading.)*

ANN.   What is it Jimmy?

BROWN.   It's a play.

ANN.   A play? What play?

BROWN.   A play. I wrote it.

ANN.   You Billy Brown? You wrote a play?

BROWN.   Ain't I say so?

PAPA SHAKESPEARE.   Billy, ya did it. Ya dey go write story 'bout dem same self people dem for go be play.

SARAH.   Girl, the man gone and wrote hisself a play. What's the story 'bout Billy? What ya call it?

BROWN.   "The Drama of King Shotaway." It's about an insurrection of the Caribs on St. Vincent Island. It's about a king, Jimmy. A Black-Carib king. A wild majestic Lord robed in the muscles on his back. Tall and strong and quick as thunder. He carries a big machete, but it ain't for to cut down no cane. It ain't no sugar juice drippin' down from he blade. No, it's blood Jimmy. Blood. Way up there on top a

Dorsetshire Hill in St. Vincent Isle, he bleed his blood for freedom. Ya see, it's them ones what willin' to sacrifice and suffer what know it. 'Cause they the ones what know what it is not to have it.

ANN. Read it to us Jimmy. Read it.

HEWLETT. King Shotaway says — "Behold these chains we wear. The shackles of our enslavers, the despotic English, who mend these merry garments with the thread of your labor and your dreams. And your children hunger for those dreams. They are weak for want of desire. Frail from wanting to see a face of a hero they could be. Blush in your shame and break with these vestments of disgrace. Spurn them with your burning indignation. Rise up naked and extirpate these despots from your world. Restore yourselves, your wives and your children to the inheritance of your ancestors, who inspire your fury and who show you the way. Those marvelous, struggling spirits who suffered to you the air you breathe; who knit time for you to walk on; who give you stars to cover your body."

END

PROPERTY LIST

ACT ONE

ON-STAGE
In big trunk:
       Jimmy's old cape
       Ann's train, string visible
       Ann's veil dressing pieces
In small trunk:
       black "corse" cover
       1 clothes brush
On overturned suitcase:
       ironing board
       1 scorch rag
       garment (fabric)
On throne chair:
       make-up kit with sponge and various bottles
On screen:
       Ann's shawl
On mirror:
       Richard III sword
       sword belt
In sewing kit:
       scissors
       ribbon
       Sarah's glasses
       darning egg and needle
       legging stocking
       needle threaded in legging
On stove:
       coffee pot with water
       kettle with water
       2 irons

On stove box:
>water basin with rag and water
>coffee grinder
>coffee strainer with pan
>2 spoons
>2nd rag
>3 tin cups on shelves

On ladder:
>clothesline with various clothes items

On Stage Left Center crate:
>2 cups

In hat box:
>1 wig block with Ann's old bonnet

OFFSTAGE
Richard III prompt script
Newspaper review
Billy's leather bag
1 Acting Company closing leaflet

ACT TWO

OFFSTAGE
Bundle with:
>new cape (on bottom)
>green tinsel in flower bag
>1 pair of leggings
>3 bundles of rags and tatters
>Ann's bonnet with red and black roses
>Papa's pigeon-tailed coat
>ballroom curtain, accordion folded
>pants

Sarah's head doughnut
King of Shotaway manuscript (diary-like)

COSTUME PLOT

ACT ONE

SARAH
>Brown lace-up ankle boots
>Ribbed tights
>Petticoat
>Green plaid skirt
>Slate gray blouse
>Wine and lavender shoulder shawl
>Gold and green plaid wool shawl with fringe
>Head wrap
>Apron
>Wire-rim glasses

ANN
>Black flat pumps with ribbon ties
>Ribbed tights
>Petticoat with butt pad
>Indigo blue floral dress
>Brown and black rehearsal train

STEPHEN PRICE
>Black ankle boots
>Gray striped pants
>White ruffle front shirt
>Ivory vest
>Blue brocade vest
>Navy frock coat with black velvet collar
>Black dotted cravat
>White gloves
>Black top hat

CONSTABLE-MAN
>Black riding boots
>Black wool pants

Black caped overcoat
Black velvet stock and collar dickey
Black beaver stovepipe top hat

JAMES HEWLETT

Black ankle boots
Brown windowpane pants
White shirt with red stripes
Caramel brocade vest
Brick red bob tailcoat
Red cravat
Black hat
Rehearsal drape with cape

BILLY BROWN

Black boots
Black and brown striped pants
Light green plaid shirt
Green and rust plaid vest
Green velvet frock coat with suede collar
Brown suede hat
Black dotted cravat

PAPA SHAKESPEARE

Brown slippers
Striped hose
Rust windowpane pants
Green plaid shirt
Red and orange ruffled skirt
Brown tweed vest
Green and blue distressed frock coat with leather
    talismans
Rust cravat with beads
Hat
Beaded necklaces

ACT TWO

SARAH
>Purple patchwork dress with smocked sleeves
>Purple embroidered cotton robe with quilted
>>sleeves and velvet ties
>
>Purple patchwork turban with black plume and
>>front drape
>
>Brown lace-up ankle boots

ANNE
>Scene 2: same as Act One, with:
>>gray sweater/jacket
>>tan knit shawl with tassel fringe
>>straw bonnet
>
>Scene 4:
>>black cotton empire dress with green embroidery
>>black poke bonnet with red roses and red velvet
>>>ribbon trim
>>
>>black veil

STEPHEN PRICE
>same as Act One

CONSTABLE-MAN
>same as Act One

JAMES HEWLETT
>Ribbed tights
>Cordovan short boots
>Red velvet pumpkin hose with white puffs
>Red and black patchwork doublet
>Red velveteen robe
>Red and gold crown

BILLY BROWN
Brown ankle boots
Ribbed tights
Blue patchwork pumpkin hose
Blue and white couplet with sleeve guards
Blue patchwork cape

PAPA SHAKESPEARE
Black, red and green patchwork robe
Black bicorn hat with tan fringe trim
Black patchwork and quilted vest

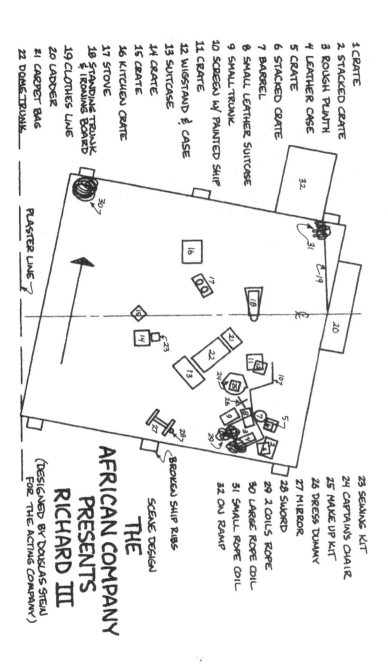

1 CRATE
2 STACKED CRATE
3 ROUGH PLINTH
4 LEATHER CASE
5 CRATE
6 STACKED CRATE
7 BARREL
8 SMALL LEATHER SUITCASE
9 SMALL TRUNK
10 SCREEN W/ PAINTED SHIP
11 CRATE
12 WIGSTAND & CASE
13 SUITCASE
14 CRATE
15 CRATE
16 KITCHEN CRATE
17 STOVE
18 STANDING TRUNK & IRONING BOARD
19 CLOTHES LINE
20 LADDER
21 CARPET BAG
22 DOME TRUNK

23 SEWING KIT
24 CAPTAIN'S CHAIR
25 MAKE UP KIT
26 DRESS DUMMY
27 MIRROR
28 SWORD
29 2 COILS ROPE
30 LARGE ROPE COIL
31 SMALL ROPE COIL
32 ON RAMP

PLASTER LINE

BROKEN SHIP RIBS

SCENE DESIGN

THE
AFRICAN COMPANY
PRESENTS
RICHARD III

(DESIGNED BY DOUGLAS STEIN
FOR THE ACTING COMPANY)

NOTES
(Use this space to make notes for your production)